REDBACK publishing

AUSTRALIAN TRANSPORT

RAIL TRANSPORT

ALISON HIDEKI

First Published 2018 by
Redback Publishing
Suite 6, 13a Narabang Way,
Belrose NSW 2085
Australia

www.redbackpublishing.com
orders@redbackpublishing.com

ISBN 978-1-761401-56-5

Author: Alison Hideki
Editor: Marianne Lindsell
Designer: Redback Publishing

Original illustrations © Redback Publishing 2025
Originated by Redback Publishing

Acknowledgements
Abbreviations: l—left, r—right, b—bottom, t—top, c—centre, m—middle
We would like to thank the following for permission to reproduce photographs: (Images © shutterstock) p5r Couple sitting in horse drawn buggy State Library of Victoria, p6 Coal train State Library of Victoria, p7m The jetty, Bulli coal mine by Robert Bruce State Library of Victoria, p10m State Library NSW Construction of Sydney City Railway 1922-1923, p11b Central Railway Station State Library of New South Wales, p11t Mixed gauge trackwork, North Geelong, Victoria, Australia by Marcus Wong via Wikimedia Commons, p11m Passenger rail map By Lencer via Wikimedia Commons, p13 John Forrest by Gordon H Woodhouse State Library of Victoria , p15b Scott Kenneth Brodie, p17m Travel by electric train to the football grounds Victorian Railways State Library of Victoria, p18t Beaumaris Tram by George Rose State Library of Victoria, p19t Sydney st tram car by Henry King State Library of Victoria, p21t NSW TrainLink XPT First Class Sleeper By Hpeterswald via Wikimedia Commons, p21m indian pacific dining car By Cheryl Cox via Wikimedia commons, p30t The Ghan by Bahnfrend via Wikimedia Commons.
Every effort has been made to contact copyright holders of any material reproduced in this book. Any omissions will be rectified in subsequent printings if notice is given to the publisher.

A catalogue record for this book is available from the National Library of Australia

CONTENTS

RAILWAYS TODAY

Australia's rail system connects most populated areas, and plays an important role in transporting large volumes of goods such as wheat, wool, coal and iron ore.

In cities, trains are a major form of public transport. In Sydney alone, there are over 1 million customer journeys per weekday, and about 325 million customer journeys a year.

POWER FOR RAIL

Railway vehicles include trains, trams and monorails. Engines with diesel or electric motors power most rail vehicles, although in the past, steam engines, horses and even people have been used to move carriages and trucks along rails.

EFFICIENT TRANSPORT

Modern trains are safe and efficient. They cause less damage to the environment than many other forms of transport, especially cars and trucks. Once the track has been laid, the cost of operating trains is low compared with other forms of transport, especially airplanes. However, goods and passengers can travel only to places with railway stations – road vehicles can travel just about anywhere.

RAILWAYS IN THE PAST

Australia's first train service began in 1854 in Melbourne. For the next 100 years, railways played an important role in the developing wheat and wool industries, and in spreading European farming and settlement throughout Australia. Trains replaced horse-drawn and bullock-drawn wagons as the main method of transporting goods overland.

Until about 1950, most people used trains to travel long distances. Then air and road transport became cheaper and more reliable, and fewer passengers used railways. The use of railways to transport freight also declined as roads improved.

TRANSPORT

Transport is the movement of people or goods from one place to another. There are many kinds of transport, including airplanes, cars, trucks, ships, trains, pipelines and conveyor belts. Transport has always been very important for humans, as it makes it possible for people to communicate with one another, and to trade with one another.

Australia's first train service commemoration stamp

THE FIRST RAILWAYS

Engines did not power Australia's first rail vehicles. Carriages and goods wagons were drawn by horses, and in some cases were pulled along by people.

COAL TRANSPORT

The first railway in Australia was built in Newcastle, New South Wales, in 1827. It was a horse-drawn railway, used to transport coal from the mine to the wharf to be loaded on to ships. After that time, railways were commonly used in mines and factories to transport goods.

They were usually trucks or trolleys, pulled by horses along iron rails. In 1854, a horse-drawn railway was opened between Port Eliot and Goolwa, on the mouth of the Murray River in South Australia.

1885, Melbourne's first cable tram service.

PEOPLE POWER

Australia's first passenger railway was built in Tasmania in 1836. Convicts pushed small carriages along wooden rails. The railway ran about eight kilometres from the port of Norfolk Bay to the penal settlement of Port Arthur. The rails were 10 centimetres high and five centimetres wide. They were made from the trees cut down to clear the route, and were nailed to rough sleepers, which were sunk into a bed of clay. Several wooden bridges carried the line over gullies as the track wound its way through rugged rainforest.

Each carriage held four passengers, and was driven by four convicts who pushed against crossbars at the front and rear. The convicts pushed the carriage uphill and along flat sections of track, and jumped aboard during downhill sections. The carriages were slowed on the downhill runs by wooden brakes attached to one of the rear wheels. At times the carriages reached speeds of about 50 kilometres per hour. The line was closed in 1877.

A small steam train leaving the jetty after loading a boat with coal.

EYEWITNESS ACCOUNT

A visitor to Port Arthur in 1851 described his journey on the convict powered railway:

'. . . they rattled (downhill) at tremendous speed, the chains around (the convicts') ankles chinking and clanking as they trotted along. (Then) the runners jumped upon the side of the trucks in rather unpleasant proximity [closeness] with the passengers . . .'

THE AGE OF STEAM

The invention of the steam engine made railways the fastest and cheapest method of land transport in the mid-to-late 1800s. Trains all but brought about the end of horse-drawn coaches, inland river paddle steamers and bullock trains.

The first steam train service in Australia ran from Flinders Street, Melbourne, to the wharves at Sandridge (Port Melbourne). The Hobson's Bay Railway Company operated it, and it opened in September 1854, carrying passengers and goods on the four-kilometre journey between the port and the city centre.

The following year the Sydney Railway Company opened a 22-kilometre line between Sydney (Redfern) and Granville, near Parramatta. Soon railways were being built between cities and nearby towns, such as Campbelltown (linked to Sydney in 1858) and Geelong (linked to Melbourne in 1859).

Steam trains were the only trains in Australia until the early 1900s when electric trains began to be used in suburban railways. Steam trains continued to play an important part in Australia's country railways until the 1950s.

HOW A STEAM ENGINE WORKS

In a steam engine, coal is burned to turn water into steam. The steam takes up more space than the water, and the force created as the steam is released is used to push pistons, which in turn make the wheels turn. Smoke from the burning coal is 'puffed' out into the air. Steam is also released.

Coal for the steam engine is usually carried in a special small truck called a coal tender behind the engine. Extra water is also carried in a tank, which must be refilled during longer journeys from trackside water tanks.

The fireman (the person responsible for keeping the fire alight and at the right temperature) shovels coal into the firebox, which heats water in the boiler. The driver controls the speed of the engine by changing the amount of steam that is released to push the pistons.

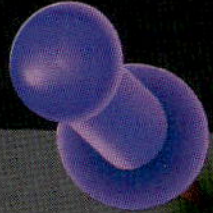

FIRST STEAM TRAIN SERVICES

DATE	COLONY/TERRITORY	FROM	TO
1854	Victoria	Melbourne (Flinders Street)	Port Melbourne
1855	New South Wales	Redfern (near Sydney)	Granville
1856	South Australia	Adelaide (North Terrace)	Port Adelaide

Stoking the furnace

THE SPREADING WEB OF STEEL

After the gold rushes (1850-1860), Australia's rail network grew quickly. Gold had brought great wealth to the colonies, especially Victoria and New South Wales. Governments had plenty of money to spend on this new form of transport, which they hoped would give access to vast areas of land for farming. Between 1870 and 1900, the total length of Australian railway lines increased from 1,600 kilometres to nearly 20,000 kilometres.

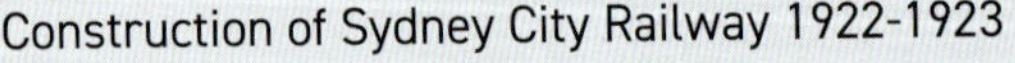

Construction of Sydney City Railway 1922-1923

ACCESS TO THE INLAND

Until the 1870s, farmers relied on paddle steamers travelling on inland rivers for supplies, and to take their goods to the cities. Riverboat trade declined as railway lines stretched into the wheat and sheep belt (a vast area of land stretching from South Australia through inland Victoria, New South Wales and Queensland).

In Western Australia and Tasmania, railways gave access to once-isolated areas for wool and wheat farming. Horses, horse-drawn coaches and bullock-drawn wagons transported goods and people from railway stations to nearby communities and farms.

Mixed gauge trackwork in Geelong

LINKING THE EASTERN CITIES

In New South Wales, rail lines were built from Sydney to Goulburn (1869) and to Bathurst (1876). In Victoria, the northern line reached from Melbourne to Wodonga on the New South Wales border in 1873. The line between Albury, on the opposite bank of the Murray River, and Sydney was completed in 1883. This linked Sydney and Melbourne, although passengers and freight had to change trains at Albury because the lines had different gauges (widths between the rails). In 1887 the railway line from Melbourne to Adelaide was completed.

In northern New South Wales, a line joined Newcastle and Tamworth (1878). This was extended to Brisbane in 1887, and in 1889 a bridge over the Hawkesbury River was built, linking Sydney and Newcastle. This finally connected Adelaide, Melbourne, Sydney and Brisbane, although the complete journey would involve four changes of train due to the different gauges.

Perth was included in the rail network in 1917 when the Trans-Australian Railway was completed.

Modern rail network Australia

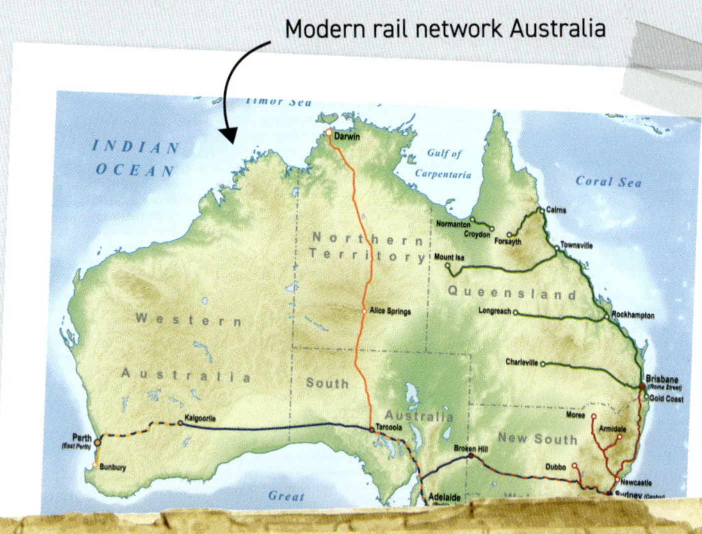

Early photo of Central Station in Sydney

ACROSS THE NULLARBOR

The Nullarbor Plain stretches more than 700 kilometres from south-western South Australia into south-eastern Western Australia. It is a huge, flat desert plain separating Western Australia from the east.

Construction of the Trans-Australian Railway across the Nullarbor between Kalgoorlie and Port Augusta began from each end in 1912. About 3,500 men worked on the track, which took five years to complete. The two lines were joined in October 1917, linking Perth and Sydney. The line was also called the trans-continental railway, because it crossed the continent of Australia.

BUILDING THE LINE

Workers cleared and smoothed the land using picks, shovels, and horse-drawn scoops. They dropped wooden sleepers and rails in place, to be fixed by a machine called a tracklayer, which was powered by a steam engine. Workers following behind the tracklayer drove iron spikes called 'dogs' into each sleeper to hold the rails in place. The gauge of the Trans-Australian Railway is four foot eight inches (1.435 metres).

Supply trains brought food, water and other supplies to the workers, who lived in rough tent towns next to the line. They moved the towns along with them as the track advanced. Conditions were harsh. During summer, temperatures often rose to 46 degrees Celsius, and in the winter, the nights were bitterly cold.

Railway construction workers laying track in the early 1900s

THE TRANS-AUSTRALIAN TODAY

The Indian Pacific rail service travels on the Trans-Australian Railway between Perth and Sydney. It is recognised as one of the world's great rail services. The 3,961-kilometre journey takes 65 hours. The line used to transport freight as well as passengers, but most passengers today travel this distance by air, and most freight is transported by ship.

Sir John Forrest, an explorer and Premier

"JOINED TOGETHER BY BANDS OF STEEL..."

When the line was finished, Western Australian politician Sir John Forrest said "From today east and west are... joined together by bands of steel, and the result must be increased prosperity and happiness for the Australian people."

John Forrest had been Premier of Western Australia when the colonies joined together (federated) to form the nation of Australia in 1901. One of the reasons Western Australians voted to join the Federation was that politicians from the eastern colonies had promised that a railway would be built from Adelaide to Perth.

RAILWAY GAUGES

DIFFERENT GAUGES

The first railways were built as separate lines with different gauges – the builders did not plan that someday the lines would be linked. The first railway in Melbourne had a gauge of five foot three inches (1.6 metres), which became the gauge used in Victoria and parts of South Australia. In New South Wales the gauge was four foot eight-and-a-half inches (1.435 metres). In Queensland, Western Australia, Tasmania and parts of South Australia the gauge was three foot six inches (1.066 metres).

WHAT IS THE GAUGE?

The distance between the rails of a railway line is called the gauge. Wide gauges are more expensive to build, but give a smoother, safer ride. Narrow gauges are cheaper to build, but give passengers a less comfortable ride as the carriages sway more from side to side.

PROBLEMS AT THE BORDER

As the rail networks spread, the different gauges became a major problem, as trains could not travel from one colony to another. Passengers had to change trains at every border, and goods had to be unloaded from one train and loaded on to another.

STANDARDISING THE GAUGES

During the 1890s, people in favour of Federation (joining the six British colonies to form a nation) argued that the rail network could help to unify the new nation. Many people argued that a standard gauge (1.435 metres) should be adopted by all colonies. However, progress towards changing the gauges was slow. In 1917, the standard gauge Trans-Australian Railway linked Sydney and Perth, but the standard gauge link between Sydney and Melbourne was not finished until 1962, and between Melbourne and Adelaide until 1995.

Today standard gauge lines link all mainland state capitals, although they are now used mainly for freight transport. Most passengers travel between states by road or by air. Within the states, there is still a mix of gauges.

STEAM DIESEL & ELECTRIC LOCOMOTIVES

A locomotive is a vehicle used on railways to push or pull trucks and carriages.

STEAM LOCOMOTIVES

Steam engines were the main type of locomotive until the 1950s. They were developed in Britain and the United States in the early 1800s, and first operated in Australia in 1854. Today some steam engines still operate on tourist lines such as Puffing Billy (near Melbourne) and the Zig Zag Railway (near Sydney).

DIESEL-ELECTRIC LOCOMOTIVES

Most country and interstate trains are powered by diesel-electric locomotives, which are usually known as diesel engines. Diesel engines are used to drive generators, which produce electricity. This is then used to power electric motors attached to the axles of the locomotive. Diesel-electric motors are more efficient than steam engines, because they do not need frequent stops for water and fuel. They also have more power at low speeds and they don't require backbreaking work feeding the coal into the furnace.

Advertising for electric trains 1935

ELECTRIC TRAINS

The electricity that powers electric trains comes directly from overhead wires. The electricity powers electric motors attached to the carriage axles. Electric trains have a number of power cars, as well as about the same number of carriages with no motors. The driver sits at the front of the leading power car. Electric trains are cheaper to run than steam or diesel-electric trains, but it is expensive to build the overhead power lines. Most rail services in cities are electric.

ELECTRIFICATION

Electrification (building overhead power lines so that electric trains can operate) of the Melbourne rail network began in 1919, and most of the lines were electrified by 1930. In Sydney, electrification began in 1926. Lines to outer areas such as the Blue Mountains and Gosford were electrified by 1960. In Brisbane, electrification began in 1979, and the first electric trains ran in Perth, in 1986. Adelaide's first electric train service commenced on 23 February 2014.

TRAMS

Trams are vehicles that move on rails set into roadways. The first trams were drawn by horses. Later, steam trams and electric trams were used. By the 1930s, trams were the most important form of public transport in many cities.

Horse-drawn tram, Victoria 1890

IN MELBOURNE

Melbourne's tram system began in 1885 when a cable tram ran from Melbourne to Richmond. A moving cable pulled cable trams in a small tunnel between the tracks. The power to pull the cables came from steam engines. Melbourne's cable tram system operated until 1940. At the same time, electric tram services developed in the suburbs. The first electric tram ran in 1889. After 1940, electric trams replaced all cable trams. Melbourne's tram network is an important public transport service today in the city centre and many suburbs.

Melbourne's modern tram service

George Street, Sydney tram 1900

IN SYDNEY

Australia's first tram service began in 1861. It was a horse-drawn service from Sydney Railway Station to Circular Quay. In 1879, a steam tram service began in Sydney, using a small steam engine pulling two carriages. Electric trams began in Sydney in 1898, and electric trams had replaced most of the steam trams by 1910. By 1933 Sydney's tram system consisted of 290 kilometres of track, making it Australia's largest at the time.

From 1939 trams were replaced with buses. The last Sydney tram ran in 1961. However in 1997, trams returned on a light rail service between the city and Lilyfield.

Light rail Sydney

IN ADELAIDE, PERTH, BRISBANE AND HOBART

South Australia's horse-pulled trams began services from Adelaide to Kensington in 1878. Later, electric trams were introduced, but buses replaced them in 1958. Today one tram service still runs from the city to Glenelg.

Trams were introduced in Perth in 1899, but were replaced by buses in 1958. Brisbane's first trams were horse-drawn. They started running in 1885. Electric trams ran from 1897 until 1969. In Hobart, electric trams ran from 1893 until 1960.

COUNTRY RAILWAYS

Today most country rail services carry freight rather than passengers, but many people still travel by train outside city areas. Governments operate main lines linking towns and cities within each state. Mining companies operate their own private rail lines to transport goods such as coal and iron ore from their mines to ports for shipment overseas. In Queensland, narrow gauge railway lines are used to transport sugarcane from farms to sugar mills.

CLOSED RAILWAYS

Some smaller branch lines have closed down altogether, while many more lines no longer carry passengers. People now travel by airplane, bus or private car. In the Northern Territory all rail services (except the Ghan service between Adelaide and Alice Springs) ceased operations in 1976. Coaches replaced all Tasmanian passenger services in 1978.

FAMOUS TRAINS

Some Australian passenger rail services have become famous. But even these services are struggling to survive as more people use aeroplanes, buses and cars.

The Queensland Tilt Train set a new rail speed record in 1999 of 210 kilometres per hour. It operates between Brisbane and Rockhampton, regularly reaching speeds of 160 kilometres per hour. It carries about 180,000 passengers a year.

The Indian-Pacific is Australia's most famous train service. It takes 65 hours to travel between Sydney and Perth, travelling through Broken Hill and Adelaide before crossing the Nullarbor Plain. The service operates twice a week.

The Ghan from Adelaide to Alice Springs is named after the Afghan camel drivers who once carried goods to outback stations. It operates twice a week, and takes 20 hours one-way.

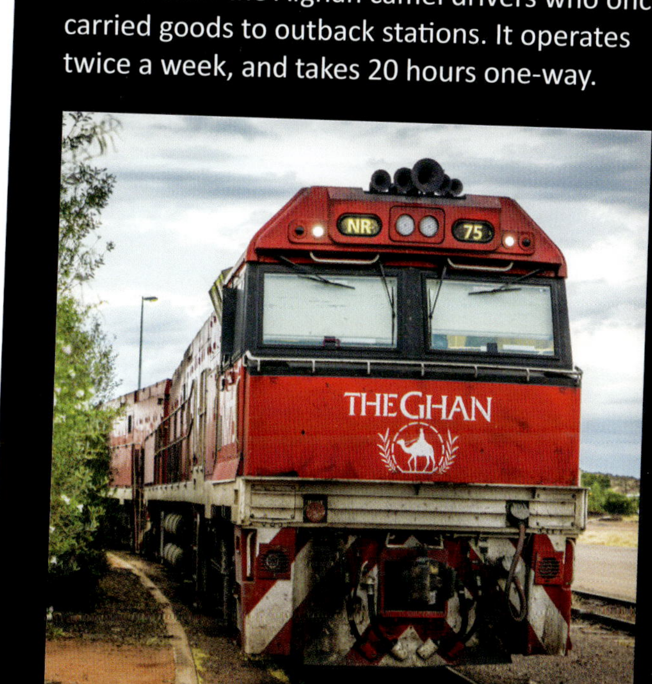

The Prospector runs between Perth and the gold-mining town of Kalgoorlie. When the first Prospector ran in 1971, it was the fastest train in Australia, reaching speeds of 120 kilometres per hour.

The XPT (Express Passenger Train) was introduced in 1982. It reaches speeds of 160 kilometres per hour on a normal trip, but is capable of faster speeds. Until 1999, the XPT held the Australian speed record for a train — 193 kilometres per hour. The XPT is used on services between Sydney and Brisbane, Melbourne, Dubbo and Murwillumbah.

CITY RAILWAYS

Australians make about 644 million journeys on city trains each year. About 203 million passengers travel on trams or light rail each year, mostly in Melbourne.

Trains in cities provide cheap, efficient transport for large numbers of people. This benefits all people who live in cities because fewer people have to drive cars. Roads are less crowded, there is less air and noise pollution, and fewer car parks and freeways need to be built. Trains are also much safer than cars.

One disadvantage of train or tram travel is that passengers can only get off at a railway station or tram stop, which may be a long way from where they want to go.

EARLY SUBURBAN RAILWAYS

In Australian cities, the earliest rail transport was horse-drawn trams. Later, train lines were built into the suburbs, but steam engines were not well suited to constant stopping and starting at suburban railway stations. Steampowered locomotives take a long time to build up speed, and so were very slow. Smoke from their engines also caused air pollution.

Electric trains can accelerate and brake much more quickly than steam engines, and do not produce smoke (although the power stations that produce the electricity cause air pollution). Electric trains started running in Melbourne in 1919, and in Sydney in 1926.

Today, about half of all peak-hour travellers to and from the centres of capital cities travel by train.

NEW RAILWAYS

Some new railway lines have been opened in Australian cities. In recent years in Sydney, a railway line was built between the suburbs of Parramatta and Chatswood, and another line has been built to link the airport with the city centre. Recently construction of new twin metro rail tunnels began deep under Sydney Harbour. The tunnels, along with some new stations are due for completion in 2021.

In Perth, a new line was opened in 1993 to serve the northern suburbs. And in Melbourne an express rail link between Melbourne Airport and the city centre is planned. Thirty kilometres of new railway line were opened in 2016 in Australia.

OUTER SUBURBS

The outer suburbs of large cities such as Melbourne and Sydney are not well serviced by rail services. This is because fewer rail lines have been built in the last 50 years, as cars have become the most common form of transport.

RAILWAY JOBS

More than 110,000 people are employed by the Australian rail sector, with many more jobs opening with demand for new rail projects.

TRAIN CREWS

Train drivers control the train. They have to keep the correct speed, obey trackside signals and stop at the correct stations. Train drivers are taught on the job. On some trains, guards travel in a carriage near the middle or end of the train. When a train is stopped at a station, the guard opens the automatic doors. He or she then makes sure all passengers have alighted (got off) and new passengers have boarded the train before the doors are closed again. Ticket inspectors work on trains and at stations, checking that passengers have bought tickets.

The train driver controls the train, obeying trackside signals. He or she must also watch for any obstruction on the track.

MANUFACTURING RAIL EQUIPMENT

Most trains, carriages and train equipment used in Australia are built in Australia. This is an important manufacturing industry.

STATION AND SIGNALLING STAFF

Major stations have a stationmaster who is responsible for running the station. Station staff sell tickets, make announcements about the destinations of trains, and help the guard of each train make sure all passengers have boarded the train safely before the automatic doors are closed.

Today many suburban and country stations are not staffed. Computerised ticket machines and recorded information are provided for passengers. Signalling staff watch train movements, and make sure signals are working properly.

MAINTENANCE AND ADMINISTRATION STAFF

Safety is very important. Maintenance crews make sure trains are working properly so they don't break down, and to limit the risk of accidents.

Maintenance of tracks and signalling equipment also prevents accidents. Worn tracks and points or faulty wheels can cause a train to derail, and faulty signals may cause trains to collide. Cleaners are employed to clean the carriages.

Rail systems are complicated to run. Administration staff work out timetables, organise regular maintenance of trains and tracks and the cleaning of trains and stations.

RAIL SAFETY

Improvements in train design, safety regulations and maintenance have reduced the number of train accidents.

SIGNALS

Railway lines have signals similar to traffic lights to control the movement of trains. When a train passes through a green signal, it automatically turns to red. When the train passes through the next signal, that signal turns to red and the first signal changes to orange. The first signal turns back to green only when the train passes through a third signal, so there are always two clear sections of track between each train.

Signal staff controls each section of track. On city and busy country lines, signal staff watch the positions of the trains on a large computer operated board. They can contact train drivers by radio.

VIGILANCE CONTROL

Some train crashes have occurred because drivers have suddenly become ill, and lost control of the train. To solve this problem, trains are fitted with devices to make sure the drivers are alert and in full control. These systems are called 'vigilance control'. On some trains, the driver pushes a button every two minutes. If the button is not pushed, an alarm sounds, and soon after the train's brakes are automatically applied. Electric trains run only when the driver holds down a handle or foot pedal. If the pedal is released, the engine automatically turns off and the train stops.

Boom gates at level crossings ensure that trains don't collide with traffic.

LEVEL CROSSINGS

In the past, many accidents occurred at level crossings, which are places where railway lines cross roads. Today, overpasses or underpasses have replaced many level crossings. Level crossings that remain are usually protected by lights and bells that operate when a train approaches, warning cars to stop. In cities, level crossings also have boom gates to stop cars crossing the train tracks when trains are approaching.

DID YOU KNOW?

In Sydney, a security control centre operates 24 hours a day, 7 days a week, with communication links to transport officers, police and emergency services. More than 10,000 CCTV cameras are utilised to monitor the Sydney Trains and NSW TrainLink Intercity networks.

THE FUTURE OF RAIL IN AUSTRALIA

In the future it is possible that Australia will have a train network that compares to other countries. In Europe, Japan, South Korea and China, trains that travel almost as fast as airplanes link many cities. In Japan, bullet trains have a system of magnets that hold them just above the rails. With minimal friction they travel very fast, very quietly and very smoothly. It is possible that in the future similar trains will travel between Australian cities. These trains will compete with airlines for intercity passengers.

The current proposal is for a High Speed Rail (HSR) between Brisbane-Sydney-Canberra-Melbourne, with numerous regional stops along the way. It would take less than three hours to travel between Sydney and Melbourne, and Sydney and Brisbane. It could carry 84 million passengers a year. However current predictions for this train being operational are for 2065.

One day travel between Australia 's major cities might take place on a train similar to Japan's Shinkansen.

Light rail systems might be extended in the future to provide an alternative to road transport in congested city areas.

LIGHT RAIL

In cities, light rail is now seen as a solution to congestion on the roads. Light rail can run on rails set into roadways like trams, and also run on separate tracks. In Melbourne, old railway lines from the city to Port Melbourne and St Kilda are now used by light rail vehicles (trams). In Sydney, a light rail service runs from Central Railway Station to the inner western suburb of Lilyfield. It uses both tracks laid into roads and disused rail lines.

Currently under construction is a light rail that will service 19 stops in Sydney's CBD and South East, from Circular Quay to Randwick. It will start running in 2019.

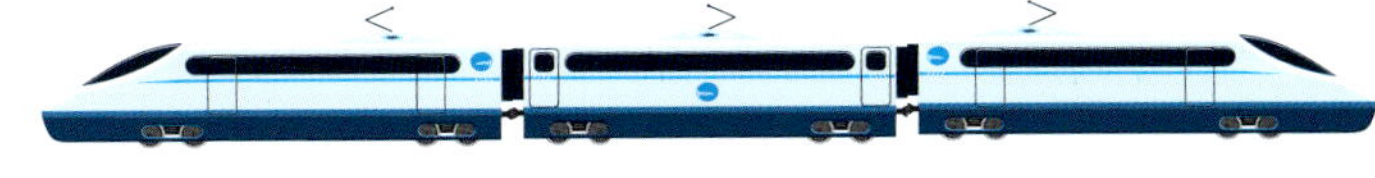

TAKE A TRIP ON AUSTRALIA'S MOST FAMOUS TRAIN

What's it like to travel on Australia's most iconic and luxurious train, the Ghan?

- When the train is fully booked, the Ghan can have 43 carriages, reaching one kilometre in length.
- The distance between Adelaide and Darwin is 2,979 km, but the trip takes 2 nights and 3 days, with stops for excursions along the way.
- On the way from Adelaide to Darwin, the train stops at Alice Springs and Katherine, and passengers can take excursions to see local sights.
- The distance between Adelaide and Darwin is 2,979 km, but the trip takes 2 nights and 3 days, with stops for excursions along the way. On-board, the train is luxurious. Passengers spend time in their cabins, or in the restaurant cars eating meals prepared by some of Australia's most experienced chefs.
- While a trip on the Ghan is expensive, it is an once-in-a-lifetime experience that many people save up for.

GLOSSARY

axle a rod joining two wheels

branch line a less important line from a main centre to a smaller town

derail leave the rails

express a train that stops only at the larger stations, and so reaches its destination quicker

fireman driver's assistant (in the days of steam trains, the fireman shovelled coal onto the fire to keep it burning)

freight goods sent by rail, road, sea or air

gauge the distance between the two rails of a railway line

goods wagons trucks for carrying freight

guard person on a train who is in charge of the carriages or trucks

maintenance keeping in good working order

monorail a train that runs on a single metal rail

paddle steamer a river boat with paddles on large wheels that are turned using steam power, making the boat move through the water

piston a disk which moves up and down inside a tube (cylinder) in an engine

points a moveable rail at the intersection of two railway tracks to allow trains from one track to join the other track

section a stretch of track between two signals

signalling staff people who operate the signals and points

sleeper a wooden or concrete beam that is a rectangular support for the rails

truck a carriage used to carry freight

vigilance control safety devices designed to apply the brakes if the driver is not in full control of the train

INDEX